ON THE BOWERY

TRANSPORTATION

A PICTORIAL ARCHIVE
FROM NINETEENTH-CENTURY
SOURCES

525 Copyright-Free Illustrations
for Artists and Designers

Selected by JIM HARTER

DOVER PUBLICATIONS, INC.
NEW YORK

PUBLISHER'S NOTE

Wood engravings, with their crisp black-and-white lines, were popularized by Thomas Bewick at the end of the eighteenth century and quickly became the favored medium of mass reproduction of artwork in the nineteenth. While there were only about 20 wood engravers in the United States in 1838, by 1870 their number had swelled to about 400. Most of them earned their living by engraving illustrations for the great periodicals of the era, *Harper's Weekly* and *Leslie's Illustrated* foremost among them. With great skill the artists rendered sketches and photographs into precise illustrations. The medium admitted a wide variety of styles from simple, bold line drawings to those so carefully worked that the effect of gradation of tone was achieved, sometimes with an impressionistic feeling.

By the mid-1880s the means had become available for reproducing photographs as half-tone illustrations, but they were both crude and expensive. It was not until the 1890s that the art of wood engraving began to be superseded by the new process. Ironically, now that the technique of the wood engraving has been largely lost, the popularity of these illustrations is reviving. Artists find the material widely adaptable to projects such as collage. Graphic designers are rediscovering how well the engravings complement typography.

Using his keen eye, artist Jim Harter has culled this selection from issues of *Harper's, Leslie's, Illustrated London News, La Nature, Scientific American* and more than eighteen other sources. He has chosen the material to reflect both the diversity of the subject and the variety of styles of wood engraving. Exercising his prerogative as an artist, Mr. Harter has also included a few illustrations that predate the nineteenth century, as well as some from the first decade of the twentieth, incorporating a modest sampling of automobiles and airplanes. The entire selection has been made to be of maximum use to artists and designers by including as many aspects of transportation as possible. For the convenience of users of this book, the images have been loosely grouped into nine categories: horse-drawn vehicles, sleighs, bicycles, trolleys, trains, cars (mostly of the early steam-powered types), ships, airships (including balloons and dirigibles) and miscellaneous transport, embracing everything from pack animals to rickshaws and impossible but whimsical conveyances.

Copyright © 1984 by Dover Publications, Inc.
All rights reserved under Pan American and International Copyright Conventions.

Published in Canada by General Publishing Company, Ltd., 30 Lesmill Road, Don Mills, Toronto, Ontario.
Published in the United Kingdom by Constable and Company, Ltd.

Transportation: A Pictorial Archive from Nineteenth-Century Sources is a new work, first published by Dover Publications, Inc., in 1984.

DOVER *Pictorial Archive* SERIES

Manufactured in the United States of America
Dover Publications, Inc., 31 East 2nd Street, Mineola, N.Y. 11501

Library of Congress Cataloging in Publication Data
Main entry under title:

Transportation, a pictorial archive from nineteenth-century sources.

(Dover pictorial archive series)
1. Vehicles in art. 2. Drawing—19th century.
I. Harter, Jim. II. Series
NC825.V45T7 1984   741.65'09'034   82-18304
ISBN 0-486-24499-7

Fig. I.

DÉMÉNAGEMENTS

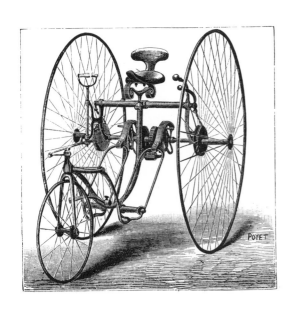

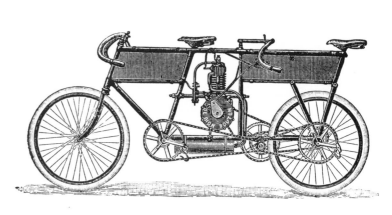

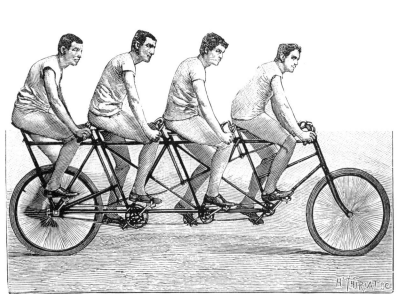

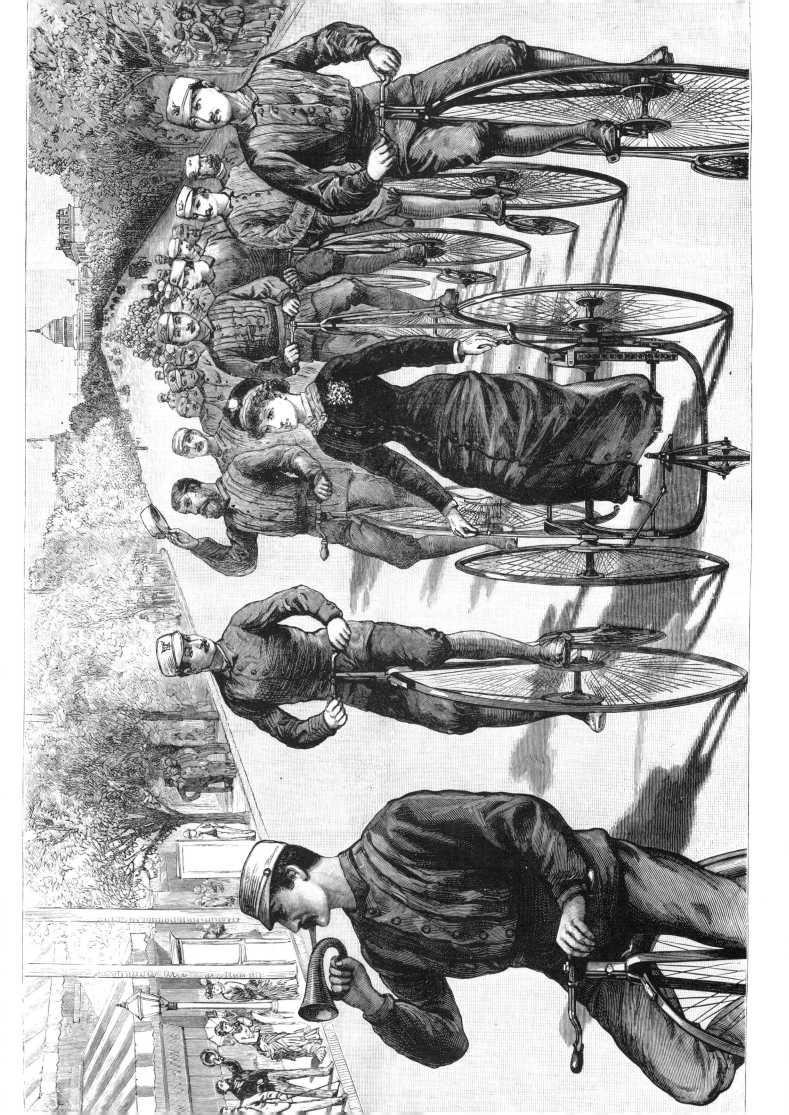

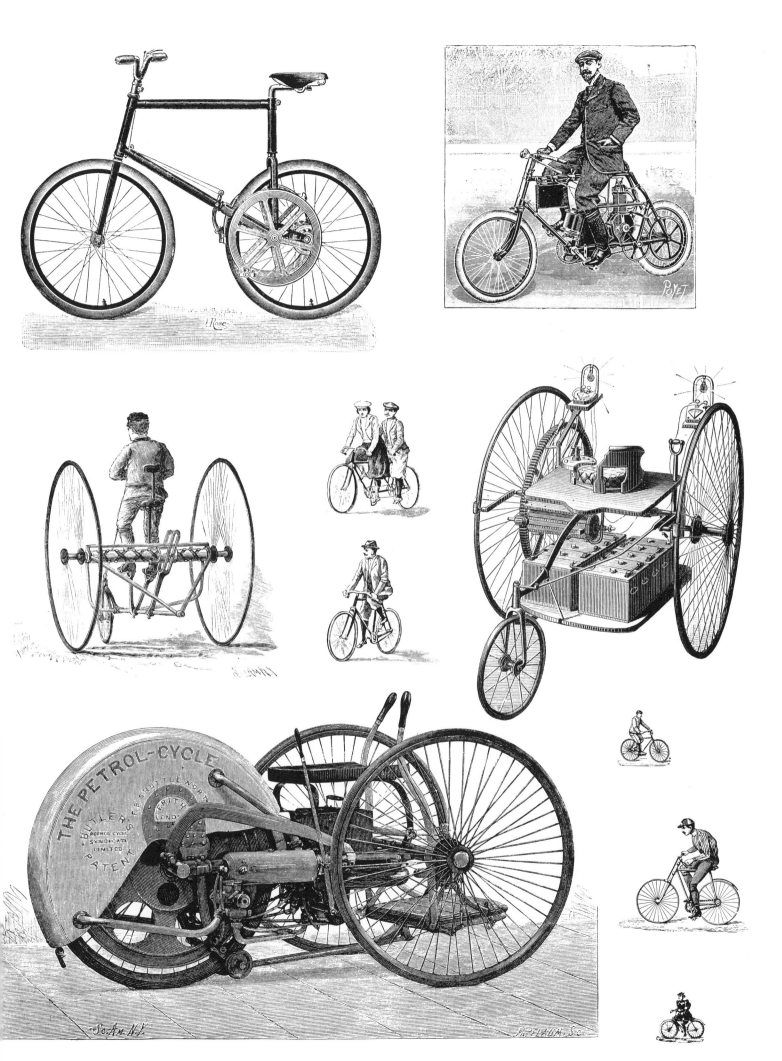

PUBLICITÉ PAR LA VÉLOCIPÉDIE · PUBLICITÉ PAR
2ᵉ SALON DU CYCLE · PALAIS DE L'INDUSTRIE · 2ᵉ S

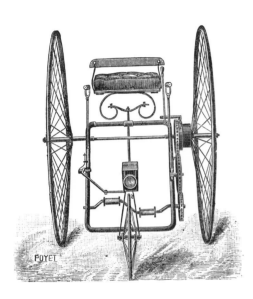

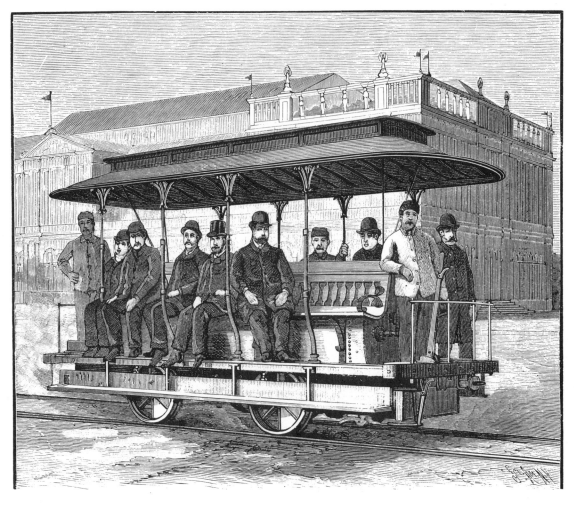

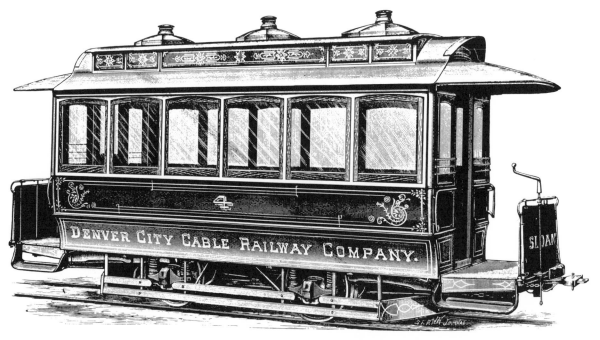

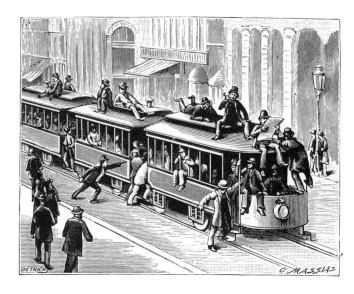

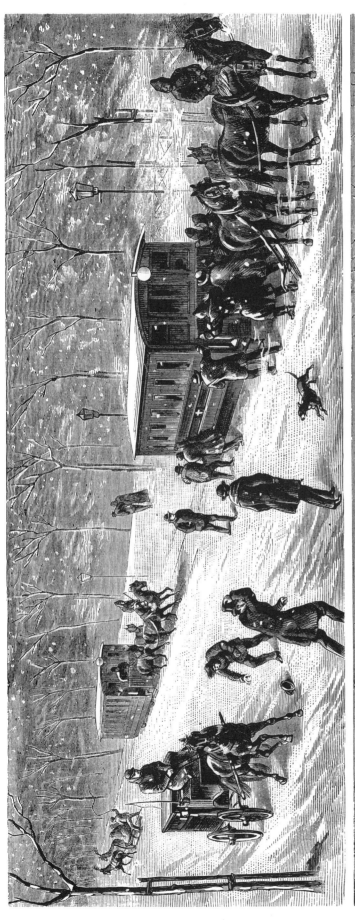

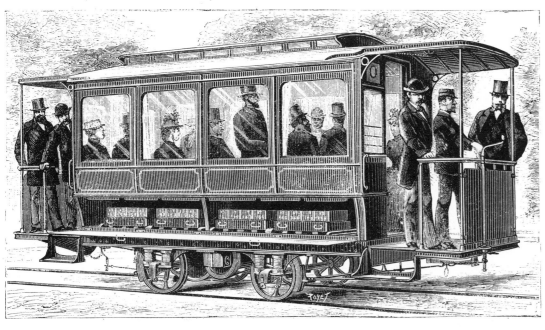

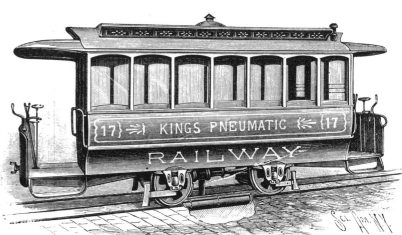

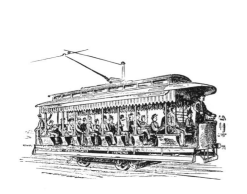

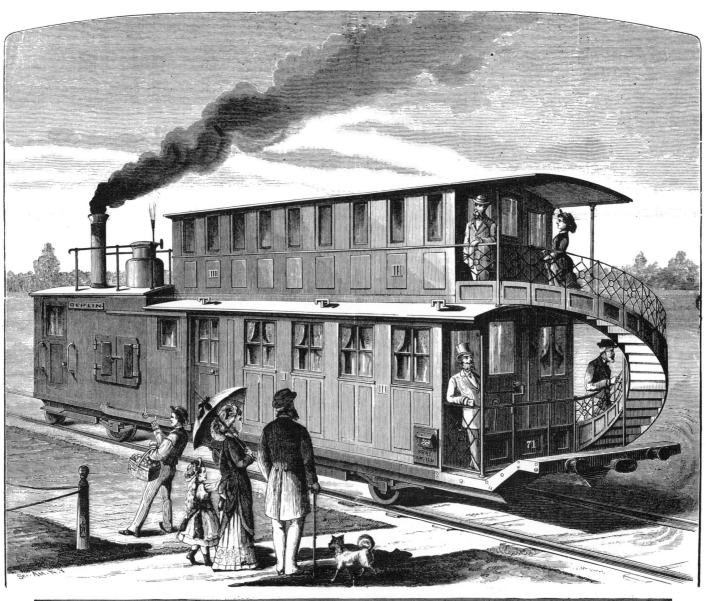

SCENE AT THE CORNER OF STATE AND MADISON. STS

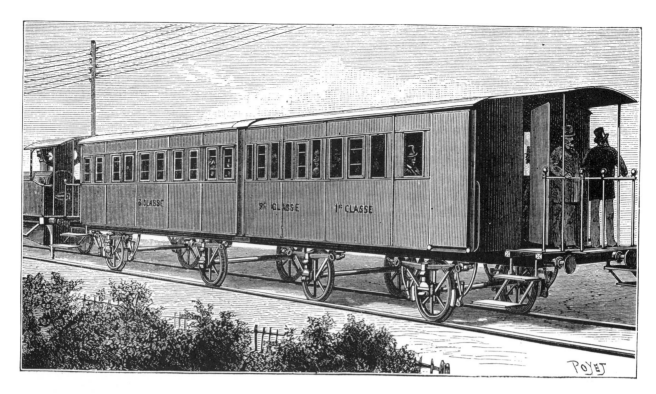

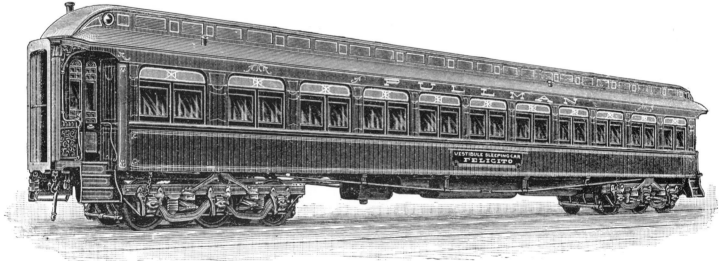

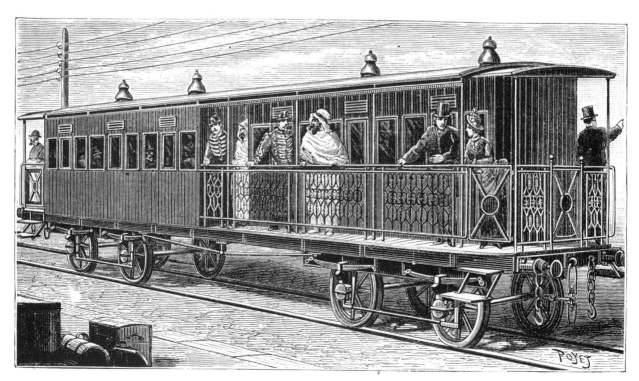

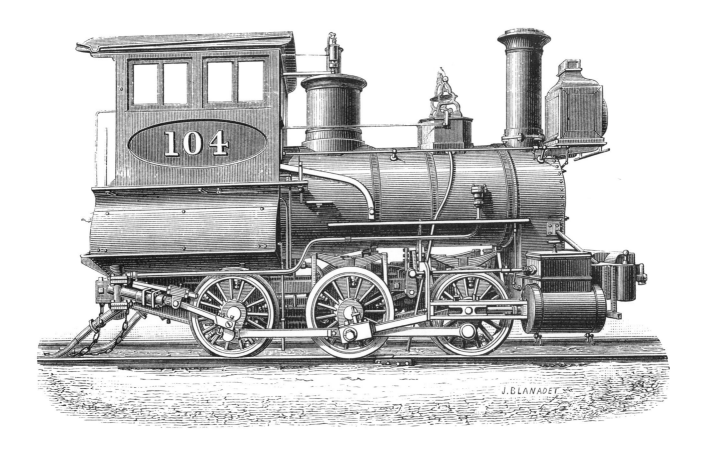

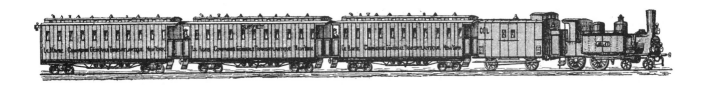

FRANKLIN SQUARE

NEW YORK ELEVATED RAIL ROAD

283

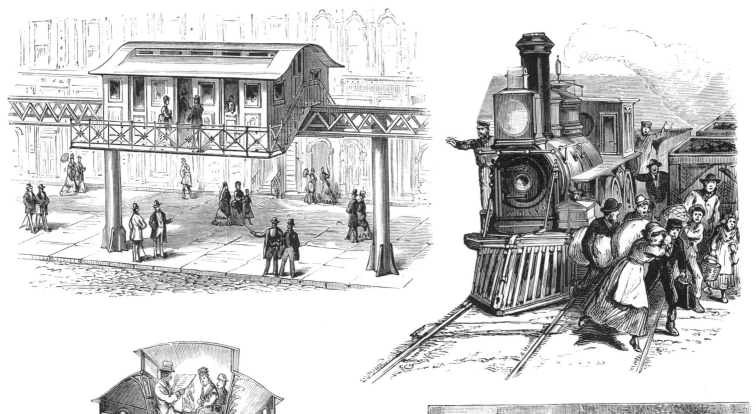

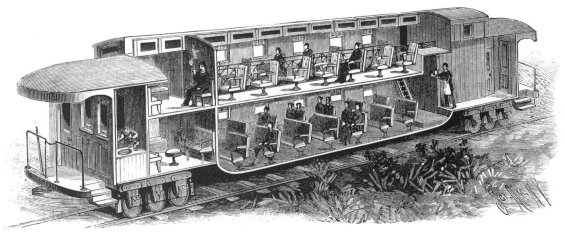

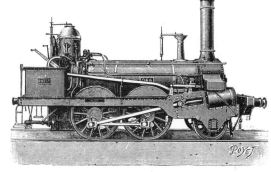

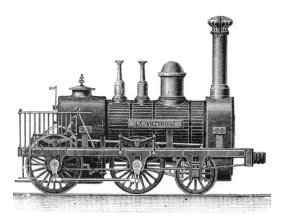

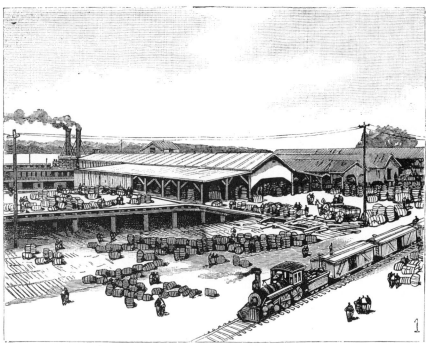

REFRESHMENTS

INSPECTOR

GOODS

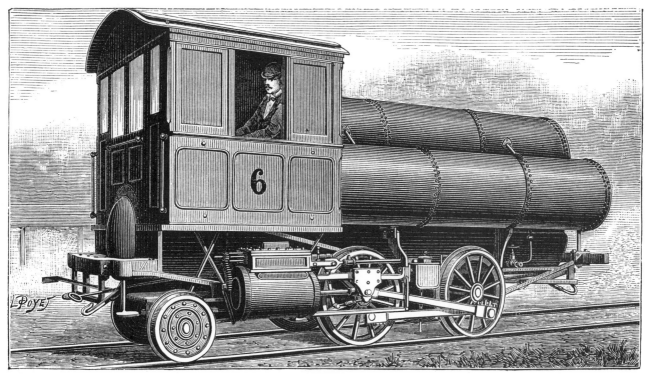

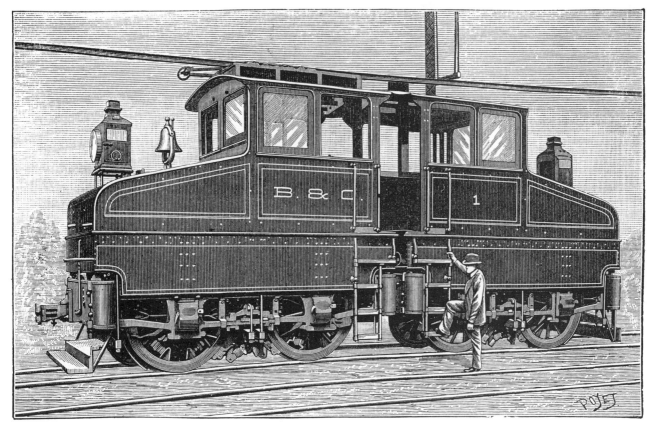

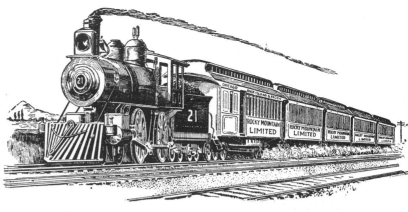

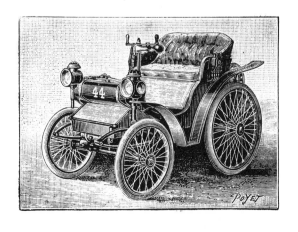

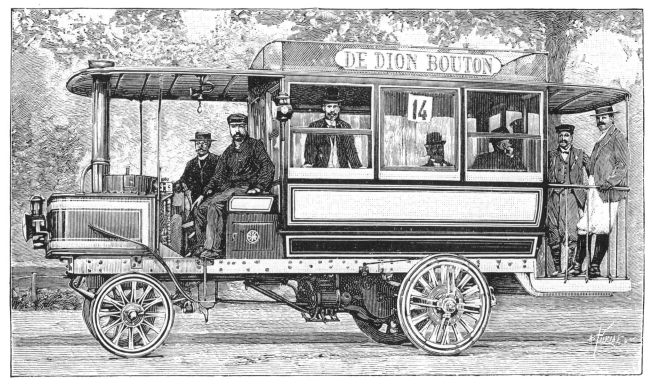

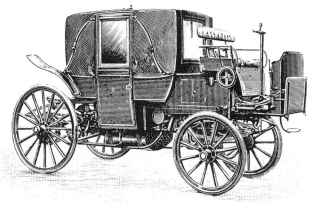

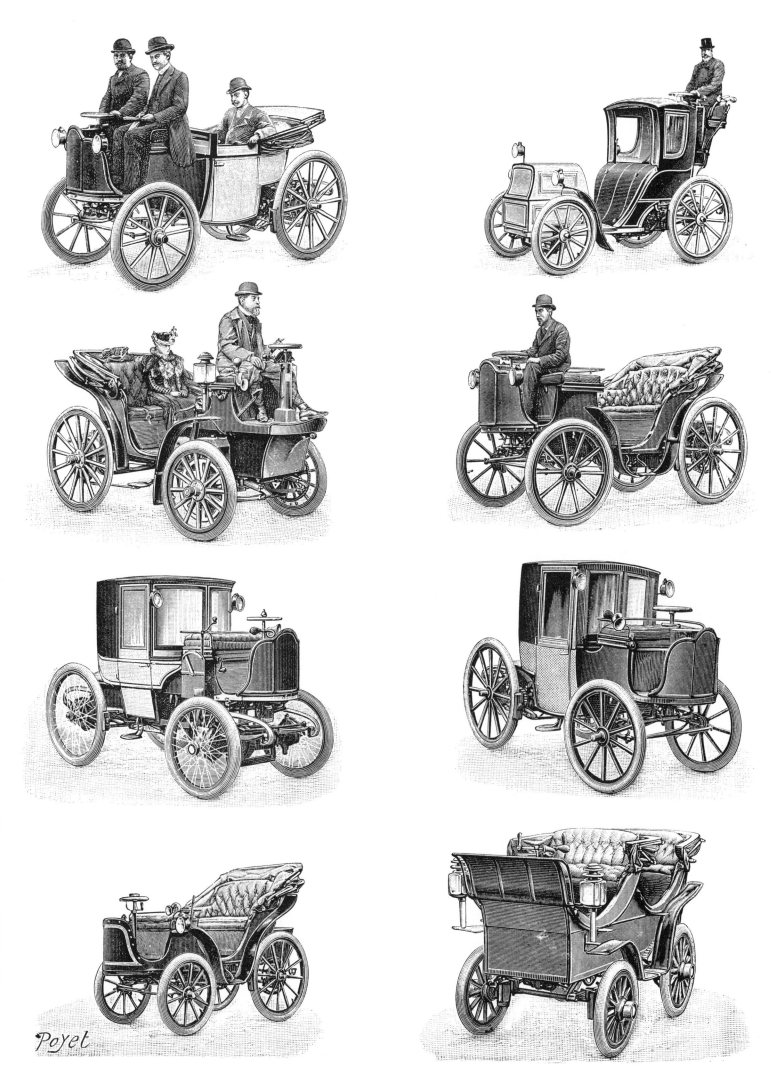

Poyet

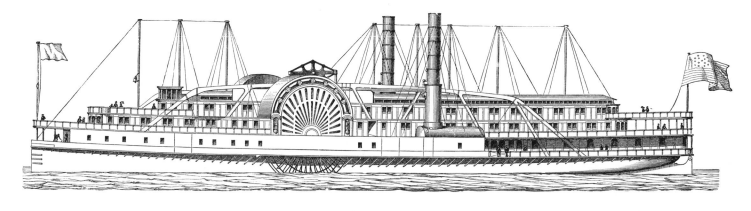

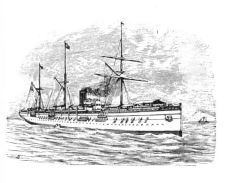

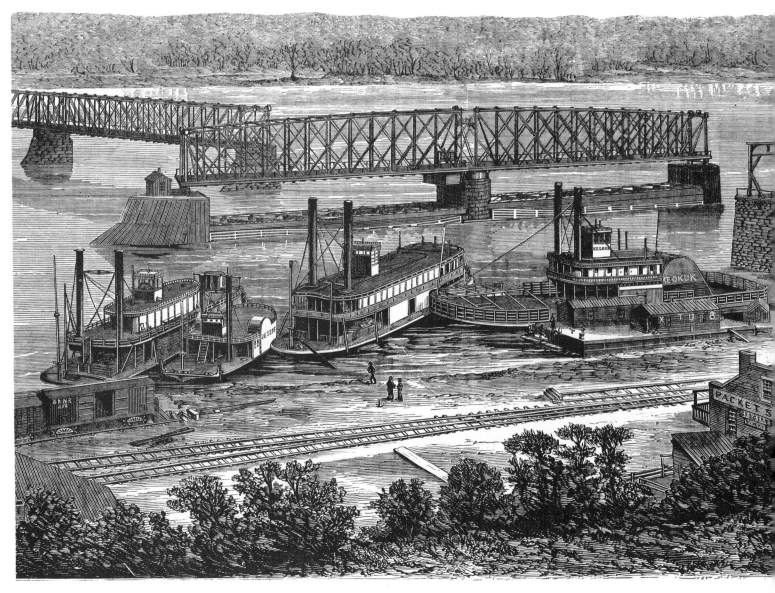

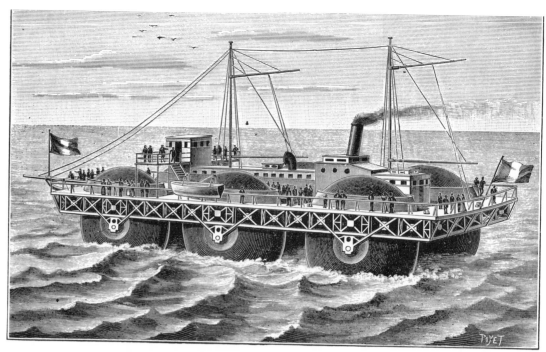

HENRY W. LONGFELLOW

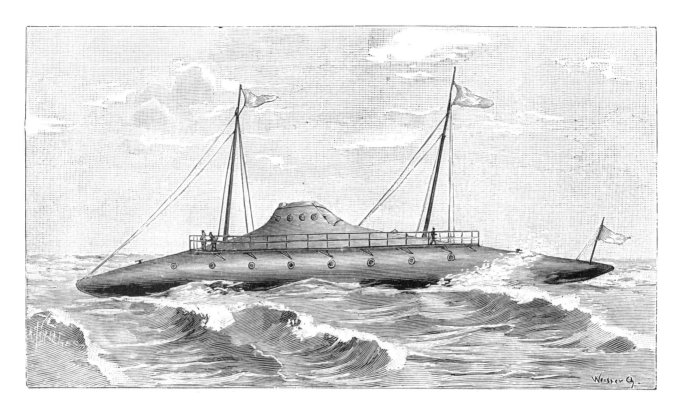

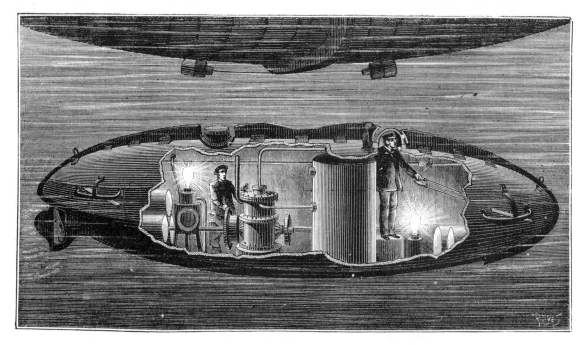

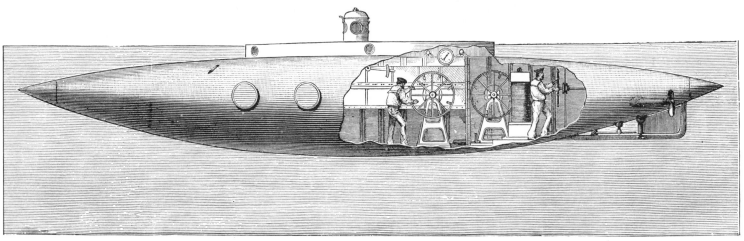

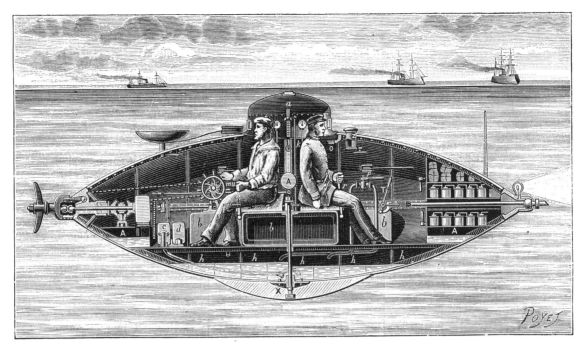

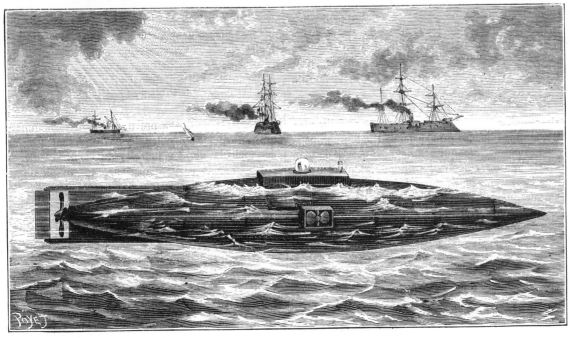

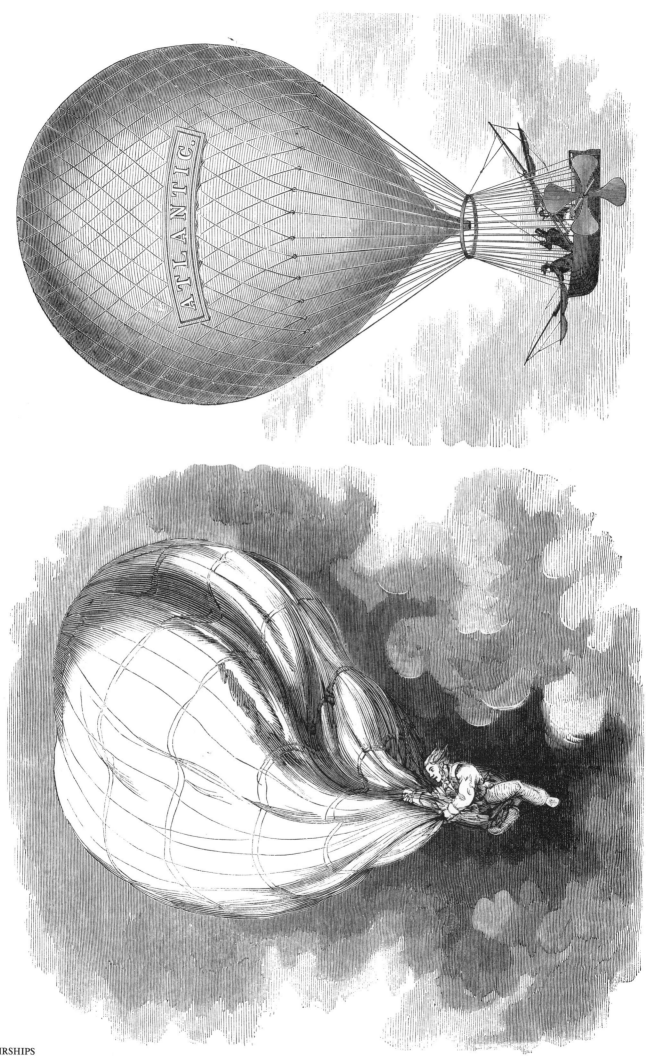

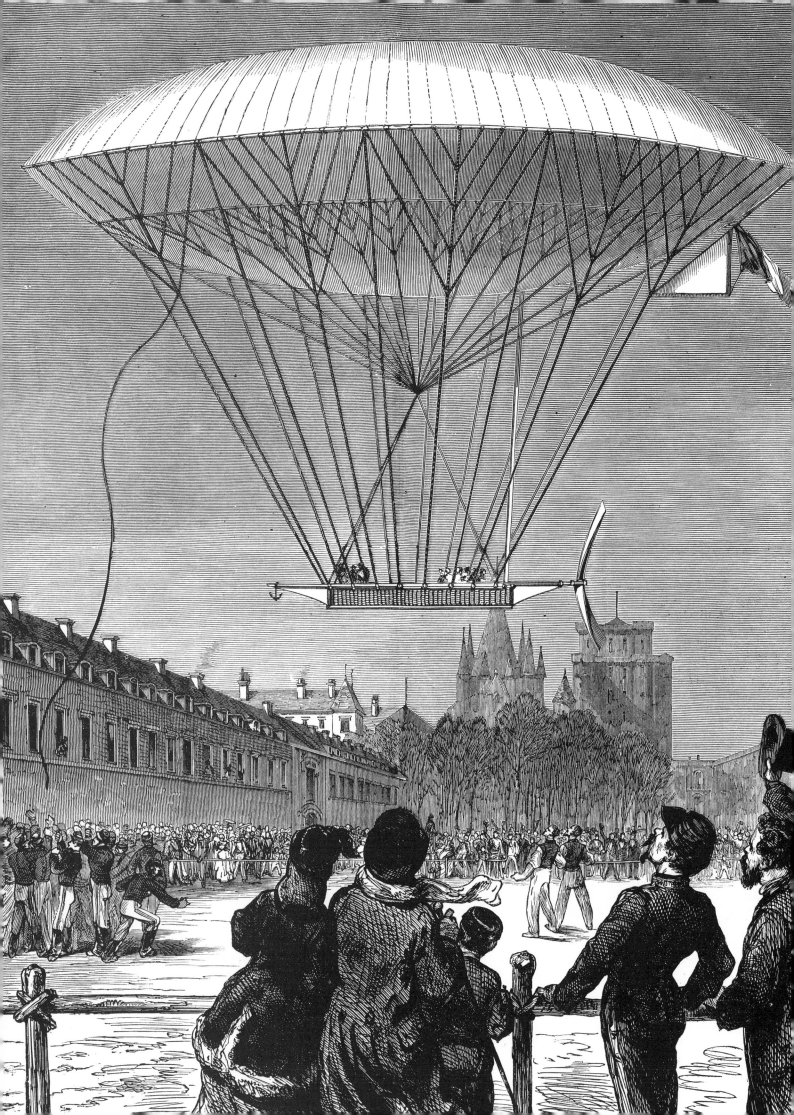

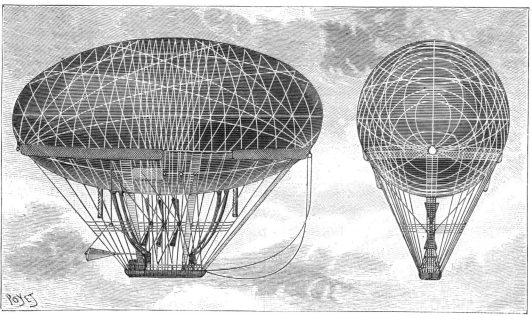

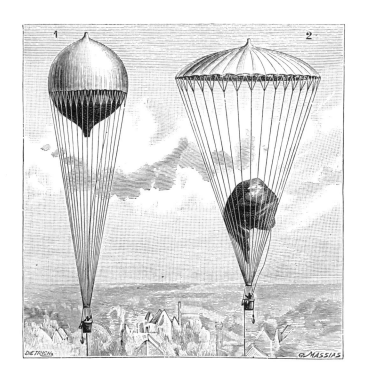

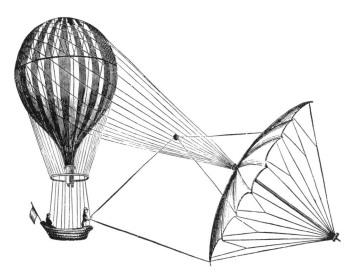

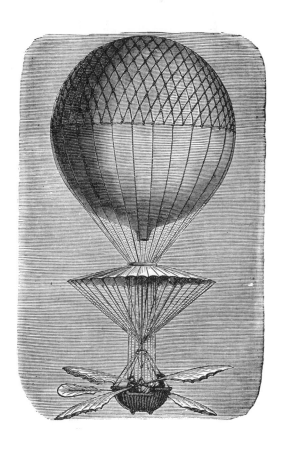

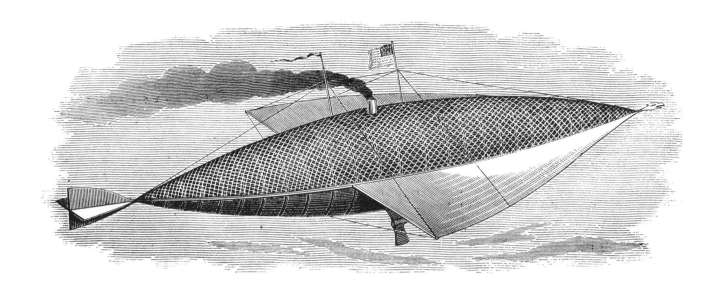

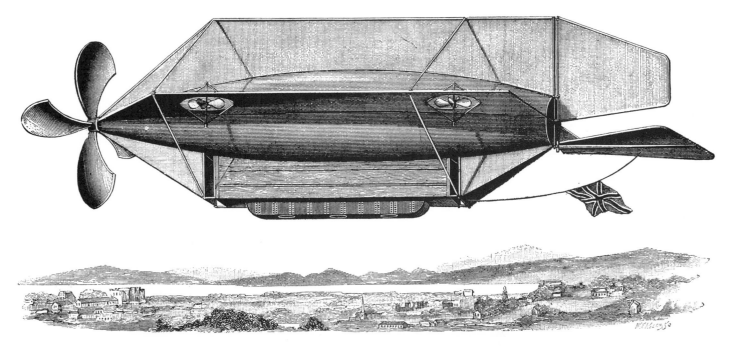

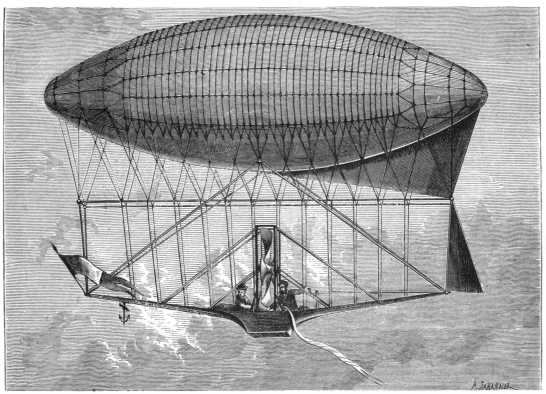

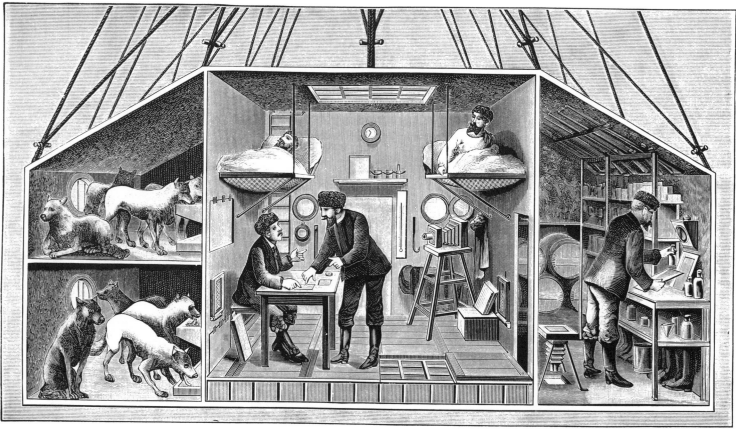

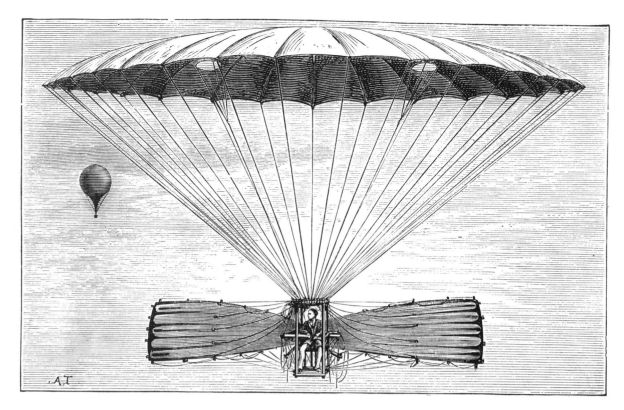

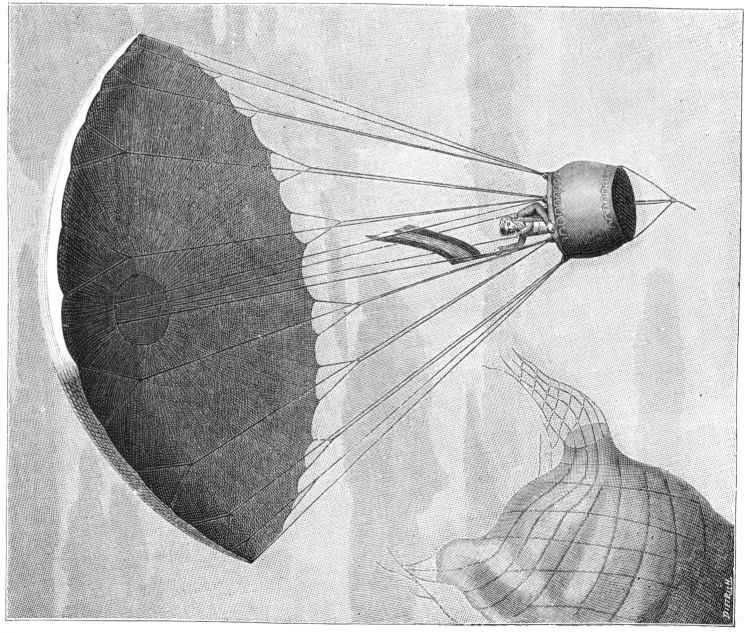

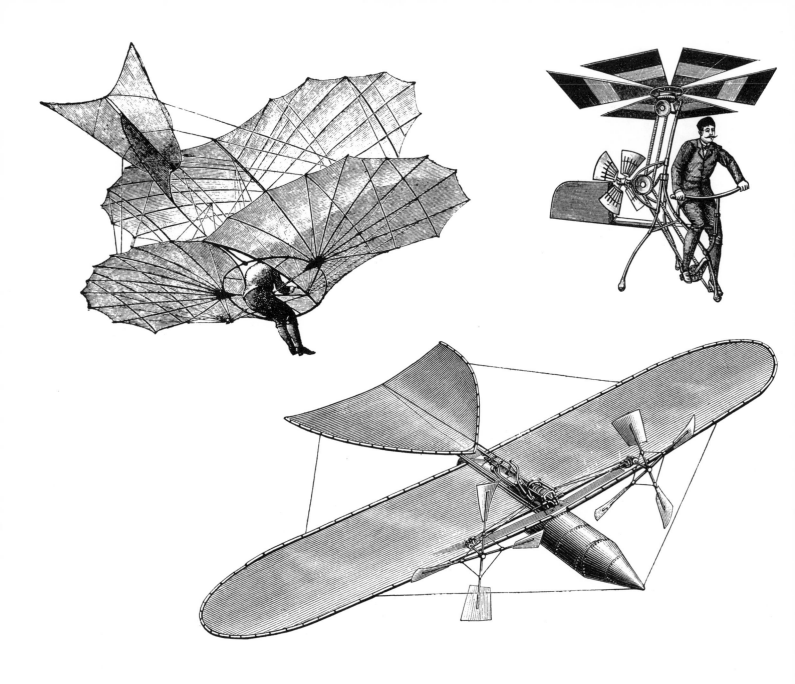

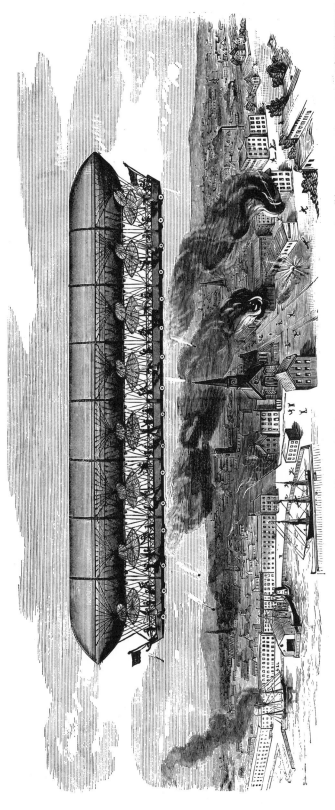

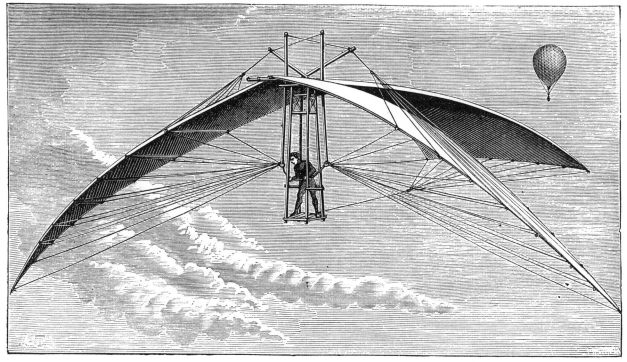

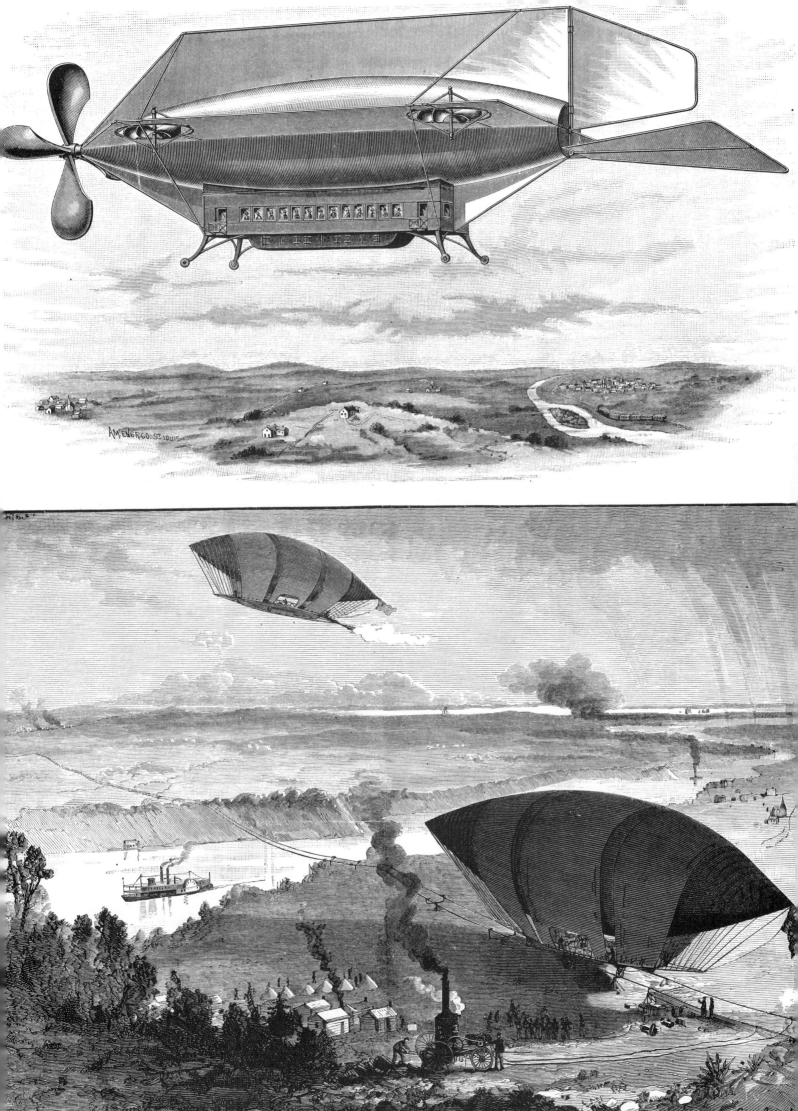

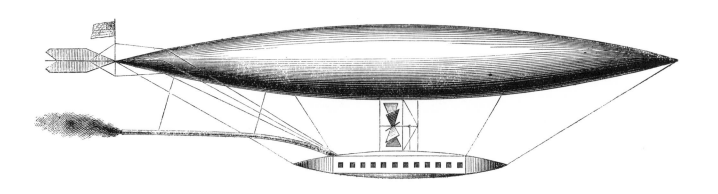

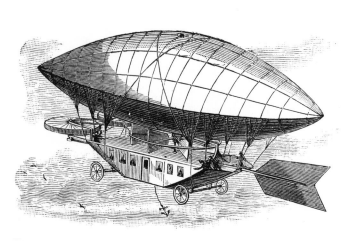

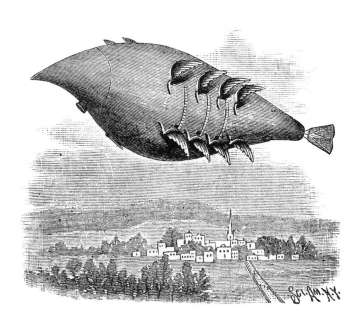

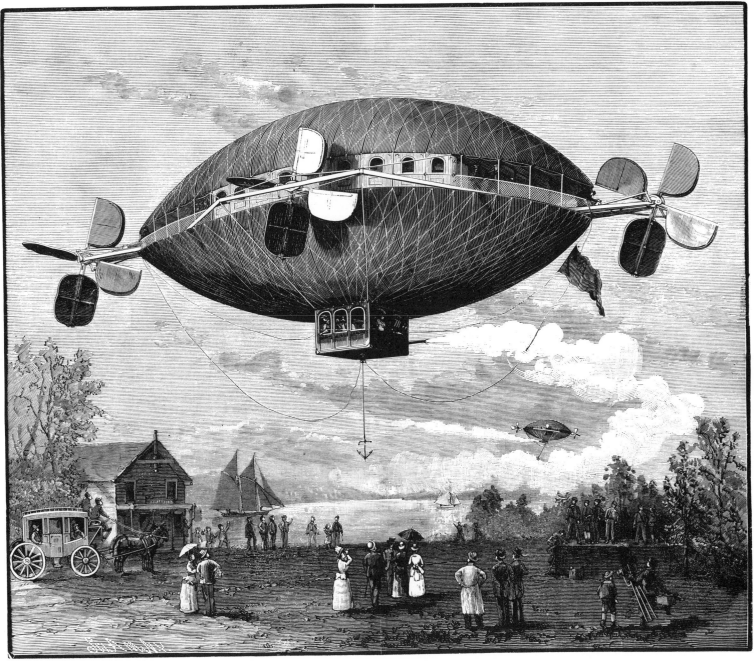